Making Summer Count

Hints for Your Best Summer Ever

— Ecclesiastes 8:15 —

And I commend joy, for man has nothing better under the sun but to eat and drink and be joyful, for this will go with him in his toil through the days of his life that God has given him under the sun.

Making Summer Count

Hints for Your Best Summer Ever

Diane E. Dunn

THREE SKILLET

MAKING SUMMER COUNT: HINTS FOR YOUR BEST
SUMMER EVER, Dunn, Diane E.
1st ed.

———————

Books by Diane Dunn:
Organizing Your Home Office for a More Successful You
Life Untangled: Living Better by Living Easier
One Layover at a Time: Tips for Traveling Well
Making Summer Count: Hints for Your Best Summer Ever

Diane's books are available from Three Skillet Publishing, Amazon, and
from Diane at her website, www.dianedunn.org.

———————

Scripture quotation is from The Holy Bible, English Standard Version®
(ESV®), copyright © 2001 by Crossway, a publishing ministry of
Good News Publishers.

Used by permission. All rights reserved.

———————

●♠● THREE SKILLET

www.ThreeSkilletPublishing.com

ISBN: 978-1-943189-83-0

A Note from Diane

Summer can be the best time of your year.

Admittedly, it can also provide pitfalls that will scramble every plan you've put into place.

How does this happen every year? Summer is something out of our regular pattern of school, work, and weekends, and we look forward to having *fun* so much that we *forget* the little chuckholes that always appear without warning.

By then, it's too late to apply the brakes, and our plans are jostled sideways, and in the worst cases, we veer totally off the road.

Making Summer Count is a roadmap of sorts. I've assembled reminders and suggestions that say, "This is a chuckhole you can avoid. Here's advance warning. Take care, and this can be your best summer ever."

So take time to look at the table of contents. See where you think you could use some pointers, and read what I have to offer. Some sections are longer than others (showing you where I've dodged chuckholes in the past), but every hint is bound to provide an option for someone to make their summer better.

I know you will think of things I haven't covered, so at the back of this book, I've provided space to write in your own hints to making your summer count. Come October, slip this book onto a shelf, ready to pull out next April. With your personal hints added to mine, every year your summer will get better and better. You will make each summer count, and it will be your Best Summer Ever.

Sincerely,
Diane Dunn
www.dianedunn.org

Table of Contents

End of School

End of School

Hint No. 1

Be Open to Changes

The month of May can be stressful with
the end of the school year and uncertain
summer plans. How you react to
unexpected changes will affect how your
kiddos will respond. Go easy on yourself,
be spontaneous, and your children will
stress less. You'll all get along better.

End of School

Hint No. 2

Before-Summer Fashion Show

To see what your kids have outgrown before summer arrives, have a fashion show. Those glitter flip-flops? That favorite swimsuit? You'll be able to tell if they fit. It might be time to head to the store.

End of School

Hint No. 3

Camera Magic

Your best summer adventures can crop up unexpectedly. Be sure you know how to access your phone's camera at a moment's notice. Document the last day of school, the outfit your child wears to summer events, and the smile you get when you treat them to an ice cream on the way home from your errands.

This -n- That

This -n- That

Hint No. 1

Sunglasses Are for Smart People

Your eyes can get sunburnt, too. Even on cloudy days, wear your sunglasses. Keep an extra pair in your car or your purse. It will be handy when you need it, and you'll save your eyes.

This -n- That

Hint No. 2

Summer Dust Buster

Little feet track in everything in the summer. Vacuum frequently to keep dust from the carpet from settling on your furniture. You'll breathe easier, too.

This -n- That

Hint No. 3

Donate the Heat

The first warm day of summer is a great time to take stock of your wardrobe. What will you really wear? Donate the rest to a charity so someone else can use what you can't while the season is right.

This -n- That

Hint No. 4

Soapy Spray to the Rescue

Fill an inexpensive spray bottle with a mix of 20% dish soap and 80% water. Use it to mist large items you need to hand wash (cookie sheets, baking pans) with soapy water, and they'll clean right up. It's also great for greasy counters or stove tops. A light spray will dispense just the right amount of soap to whisk away the grime.

This -n- That

Hint No. 5

Keeping Life Sanitary

Sunscreen and perspiration will build up on your patio furniture. Use S.O.S pads on metal. A soft scrub brush, mild soap, and a water sprayer will protect your wood and outdoor fabrics.

This -n- That

Hint No. 6

Morning "Shake-n-Go"

For those busy mornings, start off with a "Shake-n-Go" by blending 1 banana, 1 apple, 1 handful blueberries, 1 cup coconut water, 1 teaspoon almond or peanut butter, and 1 teaspoon spirulina. Prepare the ingredients the night before and pop them in the blender straight from the fridge. Leftovers can go into ice-pop molds for a cold afternoon treat.

This -n- That

Hint No. 7

Hummingbird Treats

You can keep out hummingbird nectar as long as the birds continue to visit. When they are ready to migrate, they will leave on their own. They won't stick around just because you have out food, but they will enjoy your treats as long as they stick around!

Pool Time

Pool Time

Hint No. 1

Pool Day Meals

Spending the day at the pool? Have kabobs already prepared in the fridge. When you get home, fire up the grill, and in minutes, each person has a tasty treat of their own ready to enjoy.

Pool Time

Hint No. 2

Pool Buddies

Teach young swimmers to always have a buddy in the pool. Even wading pools are deep enough for accidents. Older (and experienced) swimmers also need a partner.

Kid Friendly Zone

Making Summer Count

Hints for Your Best Summer Ever

Kid Friendly Zone

Hint No. 1

Sidewalk Chalk Ahead!

Your kids will have off days in the summer when you don't have plans and they get bored. Send them to the driveway with sidewalk chalk. You can take a good book, a glass of tea, and enjoy the time while they are occupied with their temporary art.

Kid Friendly Zone

Hint No. 2

Black Is Your Summer No-No

The sun will bake your children's black outfits during the upcoming 100-degree summer days. Try white or light blue. The paler your colors, the more comfortable you'll be. When they get dirty, they'll wash. That's what spot cleaners are for.

Kid Friendly Zone

Hint No. 3

Water Woes

Water and kids don't always mix. If you've got a water party happening on your lawn, make sure a responsible adult is assigned to supervise. It only takes an inch of water for the day to become a disaster.

Kid Friendly Zone

Hint No. 4

Save the Gas

Break out the bikes during the summer when you head to the food mart. Your kids will have a blast, and you will burn off those barbecue calories from the weekend.

Kid Friendly Zone

Hint No. 5

Chart Your Water

On hot, outdoor days, color code several water bottles for each person with permanent markers. Make sure each person drinks their share to keep dehydration at bay.

Kid Friendly Zone

Hint No. 6

Teenager Fun

Schedule several days a week for your teens' summer activities. Maybe it's just a trip to get ice cream or a bike ride in the park, but put it on the family calendar, and you'll keep your kiddos on track all summer long.

Kid Friendly Zone

Hint No. 7

Hot Seat Checkup

The interior of your car on summer days can exceed 120 degrees. Before your children buckle up, touch each of their seat belt fasteners to ensure they won't be burned.

Kid Friendly Zone

Hint No. 8

Summer Camp Ahead!

Summer camps are fun for kids. Follow the camp's recommended packing list. They've been there, and they know what your kiddos should and shouldn't bring.

Kid Friendly Zone

Hint No. 9

Taking the Red Line

Have your kids trace a train route on a map. Imagine they are on the train. What's one thing they will see? Have them write a paragraph about it from online research.

Kid Friendly Zone

Hint No. 10

Certified for Use in Aircraft

Check your child's car seat before traveling by air. Make sure it says "certified for use in motor vehicles **and aircraft**." You don't want to put a kink in your plans at the boarding gate.

Just Off the Grill

Just Off the Grill

Hint No. 1

Kid Free Zone

Summer is cookout time! Your backyard grill can be dangerous for small children. Mark off a kid-free zone with small cones, potted plants, or chairs to keep them from accidentally bumping into a hot surface.

Just Off the Grill

Hint No. 2

Crock the Pot

Meal times can be simpler with a crock pot. Start your food before you take the kids to the park, and your meal will be ready when you get home.

Just Off the Grill

Hint No. 3

Popsicle Blast

Popsicles are summer perfection. Make your own with emptied and washed yogurt containers and wooden sticks. Dip the frozen containers in warm water, and your popsicles will pop right out.

Just Off the Grill

Hint No. 4

Campout Craft

Campfires are a big draw on campouts. Assign one child a water bucket and the other a shovel. They are responsible (under adult supervision) to douse the coals when the night is through.

Just Off the Grill

Hint No. 5

Pack Your Fridge

Make sure your fridge is loaded with quick-to-fix lunch items. Cold cuts, jelly (for PB&Js) and bottled water will keep your little ones satisfied. Try preparing your bread and peanut butter ahead and storing it in the fridge to give your sandwiches a cool "snap" when your kiddos dig in their teeth.

Just Off the Grill

Hint No. 6

Prepping for a Garden Party

Hose down the walks and furniture. If the day is warm, power wash outdoor fabrics early in the day, then set them in the sun for a fresh, clean smell. Adding garden flowers to water-filled vases just before guests arrive will make your garden pop with "Wow" appeal.

Just Off the Grill

Hint No. 7

Save that Siding

Grills and siding don't mix well together. When you fire up the grill, put some space between it and your siding (or windows or plantings). You'll save your siding and have a better cookout.

Just Off the Grill

Hint No. 8

Grill Etiquette

Offer to bring a bottle of propane to the cookout (or a bag of charcoal). Bring rubber gloves and an S.O.S. pad, and jump in to help with clean up. Your help might be turned down, but the offer will be appreciated.

Around Town

Around Town

Hint No. 1

Seat Belt Safety

Summer trips are daily events. With the kids in tow, put your eye on every seat belt before you start the car. Make it a ritual. You can double-check by calling each child's name and having them reply, "Seat belt locked."

Around Town

Hint No. 2

Fire Extinguisher on Board

Heading out of town? A small fire extinguisher in your car can prevent a minor issue from crippling your trip. Keep extra water also in case you get stranded on the side of the road.

Around Town

Hint No. 3

Eyes on the Back Seat

Set your purse or briefcase (or some other essential item) in the back seat when you take trips with kids or pets. You'll be forced to check the back of the car, and no one will get left inside.

Around Town

Hint No. 4

Empty Car Policy

Make it a summer thing for everyone to exit the car with the driver. Every time. Heatstroke can happen in minutes, especially in young children. The inconvenience is worth it.

On the Road

On the Road

Hint No. 1

Out-of-Town Time

Walk your yard if you're headed out of town. See it the way others might, and secure items that could go missing. Thieves like houses that are easy targets. Don't be one.

On the Road

Hint No. 2

Stacation or Vacation, Be Prepared

You love privacy, and so do thieves. Before heading out of town, walk along the sidewalk and view your house critically. Are there places a thief could hide while breaking into your home? Get out the pruning shears and start snipping for a safer, more secure summer.

Taming the Electric Bill

Taming the Electric Bill

Hint No. 1

Watch Those Electric Rates

On a sunny day, turn off interior lights and check around your exterior doors for light leakage. Visible light means cracks, which equals dollars seeping through. Seal the crack and your electric rates will go down like a deflated balloon.

Taming the Electric Bill

Hint No. 2

Ceiling Fan Mania

Protect your summer electric bill by turning on your ceiling fan. You can adjust the thermostat and feel just as comfortable. Don't forget to turn off the fan when you leave the room. The air movement cools you, not the room.

Taming the Electric Bill

Hint No. 3

Water Heater Wisdom

You'll hardly notice a lower water heater temperature setting, except on your electric bill. Your hot water is nearly 20% of your total electric charge each month. 120 degrees is about right for most households.

Taming the Electric Bill

Hint No. 4

Let Your Dishwasher Breathe

Instead of running the heated dry cycle on your dishwasher, prop the door open and let it air dry. You'll notice the difference on your summer electric bill, not on your dishes.

Taming the Electric Bill

Hint No. 5

Blinds, Not Blinded

Block the sun with thick blinds or heavy window coverings to keep out the sun's heat. You can take off your sunglasses now. You're Welcome!

Taming the Electric Bill

Hint No. 6

Summer Energy Audit

Your power company or city specialist will usually offer you a home energy audit for free. They will suggest ways to cut energy use and can even suggest resource programs that will come to your house to do energy-related upgrades for you, often for a token amount (or even free).

Taming the Electric Bill

Hint No. 7

Save the Hot Water

Short showers are a great summer alternative to baths. Your water heater will run less, and your bill will tumble like a stone.

Taming the Electric Bill

Hint No. 8

How's Your Attic Door?

Attics can reach 130 degrees or more on sunny summer days. Check your weather stripping around your attic entrance. Heat can break down the rubber. Replacing it is easy with a repair kit from your big-box home store.

Taming the Electric Bill

Hint No. 9

Cutting the Heat

Even curling irons, stereos, and televisions add to the heat load your air conditioner must cool. The more electrical appliances you can avoid using during the hottest part of the day, the less hard your air conditioner will have to work.

Taming the Electric Bill

Hint No. 10

Wash Your Hands in Cold

Summer water temperature from the faucet is generally warmer than in winter. Make a practice to wash your hands in cold water during the summer months. You'll feel cooler, and your electric bill will be grateful.

Taming the Electric Bill

Hint No. 11

Energy Star

Look for the Energy Star label on products that use electricity. An affordable way to do this is with light bulbs. The Energy Star assures the most efficient use of your electric dollar when you flip your switches.

65

Taming the Electric Bill

Hint No. 12

Turn on the Fan

Always use the bathroom exhaust fan if you have one. The extra humidity makes your air conditioner work harder which costs you money. Check to see that your fan exhausts outside, not just into the attic.

Taming the Electric Bill

Hint No. 13

Open Blind Policy

Opening your blinds is a great way to avoid using artificial lighting. Make it a policy to close the blinds as soon as sunlight hits your windows. Your air conditioner will run less, and you'll have a cheaper bill at the end of the month.

Taming the Electric Bill

Hint No. 14

Too Simple to Be Believed

The refrigerant line between your house and your outside cooling unit needs a "line cozy." Wrap it with foam insulation, and your inside unit will blow colder, and your electric bill will be happier.

Yard Perfect

Yard Perfect

Hint No. 1

Green Up the Yard

With a little fertilizer, your grass is ready to take on your summer activities. A good way to know if you've watered it in enough is to look for visible remaining granules. If you can still see them, they can "burn" your grass by drawing water out of the grass blades.

Yard Perfect

Hint No. 2

Razorburned Lawn

After you mow, stand a ruler in the grass. Is it less than two inches? You may need to adjust the settings on your mower. Less than two inches causes the grass to need more water and doesn't give it enough "leaf" exposure to manufacture adequate chlorophyll.

Yard Perfect

Hint No. 3

Potted Peat

Add peat moss to the tops of your container plants or work it into the soil. The peat looks great and works to conserve moisture. It's great for flowers or fruit vines that need acidic soil.

Yard Perfect

Hint No. 4

Toss Thirsty Weeds

As the days heat up, your garden plants will require more water. So will your weeds. Cut the competition and cut your water bill by weeding often (daily if you can).

Yard Perfect

Hint No. 5

Wriggling in Water

Your garden flowers and shrubs like an occasional soaking during summer's heat. Leave a hose trickling at the plant's base. When the ground around the plant is soft, it's time to move the hose. In dry weather, you may need to leave the hose for an hour or more, but your plants will thank you.

Yard Perfect

Hint No. 6

Spice Up Your Landscape

Once your spring bloomers switch to summer mode, your garden can take on a monochromatic green palette. Set out a few containers in prime viewing locations. A bright planting in each one will liven your landscape with easy-care color.

Yard Perfect

Hint No. 7

Easy Weed Removal

Turning over the soil is a simple way to keep weeds from overtaking your planting beds. You'll disrupt the seedlings' growth cycle, and you'll have fewer weeds to pull.

Yard Perfect

Hint No. 8

Nature's Air Conditioning

Plants can reduce the outdoor temperature by as much as 20 degrees. Enjoy your summer under an arbor covered with flowering vines, or plant a tree that will shade your patio. You'll be cooler, and you'll enjoy your outdoor time more.

Yard Perfect

Hint No. 9

Planting an Edible Garden

Plant tomatoes, lettuce, and strawberries in with your annuals. Layer them by size, and you'll not only enjoy viewing your planting beds, you'll eat out of them, too.

Yard Perfect

Hint No. 10

Replace Drooping Plants

Not every plant will survive summer's heat well. Take a snapshot of fading plants with your phone, and you'll know exactly what to look for at the garden store.

Yard Perfect

Hint No. 11

Tackling the Big Things

Don't let July put you off from taking on major garden projects. You can lay that new patio, install that new drain, or finish out your fence with plenty of preparation. A wheelbarrow of bottled water piled with ice, a tube of sunscreen, and plenty of moist towelettes will keep you going in the hottest weather.

Yard Perfect

Hint No. 12

Coming Up Carrots

Mid-summer is the time to plant your fall carrots. The tops are lacy and will form a beautiful border to soften your faded spring plantings. Next fall, you can pull them for the dinner table.

Yard Perfect

Hint No. 13

Keep Picking!

Your food crops will produce more if you harvest often. Pole beans, zucchini, and similar crops love to put out for you. Share your excess and your neighbors will love you.

Yard Perfect

Hint No. 14

Polyfoam Pots

Polystyrene foam is a good choice if you have plants that might need moved for sun exposure. Fabric planter bags and fiberglass are also good lightweight choices.

Yard Perfect

Hint No. 15

Container Garden Choices

Your pots are an important aesthetic choice in a container garden. Remember to buy pots a size larger than you think you'll need. Smaller pots hold less soil and need more frequent watering.

Yard Perfect

Hint No. 16

Space Matters

When repotting your summer plants, don't skimp on soil. Filler material in the bottom of the pot restricts the plant's root growth and will require more water and more frequent repotting.

Yard Perfect

Hint No. 17

Your Thirsty Lawn

Some days your grass will cry out for water. You can indulge yourself, but only in the morning or the evening. Leave your lawn alone in the heat of the day or if it won't have time to dry before dark. At those times, water is not your lawn's best friend.

Yard Perfect

Hint No. 18

Dead-head Faded Blooms

Fading blooms still require nourishment from your plant. Pinch them off to encourage more blooms for better beauty. (Especially important for roses!) Your garden will pop even in the hottest season.

Yard Perfect

Hint No. 19

Ripe Fruit Bonanza

Check your fruiting vines, shrubs, and trees often. Damaged fruit won't recover and will drain water from the plant. Ripe fruits need to come off so the mother plant can give all its energy to helping the rest of the fruit ripen.

Yard Perfect

Hint No. 20

Timing Your Oil Sprays

Oil sprays in the garden are a great alternative for pest control, but only use them when it's cool. Early morning is best, otherwise the sun can burn the leaves.

Yard Perfect

Hint No. 21

Two-a-Days Aren't Just for Football

Container plants dry more quickly than those in the ground. During August and early September, you may need to water in the morning and in the late afternoon. Look for wilted or brown-edged leaves.

Yard Perfect

Hint No. 22

Shake, Rattle, and Roll

After a summer of high-traffic use, tightly packed mulch can keep water from reaching your plant's roots despite its benefits in retaining moisture. Use a garden rake to gently work the mulch loose before you water.

Yard Perfect

Hint No. 23

Indicator Plantings

Choose a plant that droops its leaves when it needs water, and plant it among your favorite flowers and shrubs. Cucumber or squash is a good choice. Their big leaves wilt easily, and you'll know it's time to water.

Yard Perfect

Hint No. 24

Becoming a Morning Person

Examine your garden first thing. Many plants will wilt under the sun's assault. If the leaves are fine in the morning, they will probably make it until evening without additional water. Only water if they are wilted before the sun hits them.

Yard Perfect

Hint No. 25

Feeding Your Leaves

Trees absorb the lion's share of nutrients and can keep smaller plants from getting enough nourishment. Use a spray-on fertilizer your flowers and fruiting plants can absorb directly through the leaves.

Yard Perfect

Hint No. 26

Your New Fall Color

It's time to renew the garden with color. Remember, the September sun can still be intense, so protect fresh plantings with shade cloth or leafy branches until they are established.

Yard Perfect

Hint No. 27

Keeping Your Garden Vital

Feed individual flowering plants or food crops directly through the roots. Use a powdered fertilizer mixed in water, and let it soak in at the base of the plant. It will green up with new vigor within a week.

Yard Perfect

Hint No. 28

Time for a Trim

Faded perennials should be cleaned and seed pods removed. The final blooms of the season will continue to pop with color when they have less competition.

Your

Summer Hints

_____

_____

_____

_____

_____

_____

— Space for Your Summer Hints —

_____

_____

_____

_____

_____

_____

_____

_____

_____

_____

_____

— Space for Your Summer Hints —

_____

_____

_____

_____

_____

_____

_____

_____

_____

_____

_____

_____

— Space for Your Summer Hints —

_____

_____

_____

_____

_____

_____

_____

_____

_____

_____

_____

_____

— Space for Your Summer Hints —

_____

_____

_____

_____

_____

_____

_____

_____

_____

_____

_____

_____

— Space for Your Summer Hints —

_____

_____

_____

_____

_____

_____

_____

_____

_____

_____

_____

_____

_____

— Space for Your Summer Hints —

_____

_____

_____

_____

_____

_____

_____

_____

_____

_____

_____

_____

— Space for Your Summer Hints —

_____

_____

_____

_____

_____

_____

_____

_____

_____

_____

_____

_____

— Space for Your Summer Hints —

_____

_____

_____

_____

_____

_____

_____

_____

_____

_____

_____

_____

— Space for Your Summer Hints —

_____

_____

_____

_____

_____

_____

_____

_____

_____

_____

_____

— Space for Your Summer Hints —

_____

_____

_____

_____

_____

_____

_____

_____

_____

_____

_____

_____

— Space for Your Summer Hints —

_____

_____

_____

_____

_____

_____

_____

_____

_____

_____

_____

— Space for Your Summer Hints —

_____

_____

_____

_____

_____

_____

_____

_____

_____

_____

_____

_____

— Space for Your Summer Hints —

_____

_____

_____

_____

_____

_____

_____

_____

_____

_____

_____

— Space for Your Summer Hints —

_____

_____

_____

_____

_____

_____

_____

_____

_____

_____

_____

— More Space for Your Summer Hints —

Turn the page to find more books

by Diane Dunn

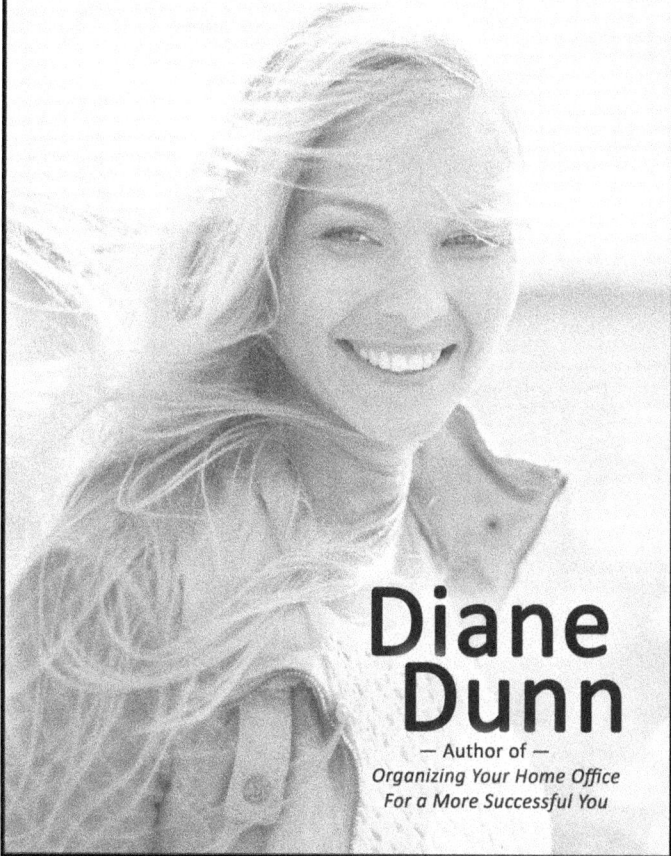

— You will look forward to your next journey! —

One Layover
at a
Time
— • —

Tips for Traveling Well

Diane
Dunn

— Everything will be at your fingertips! —

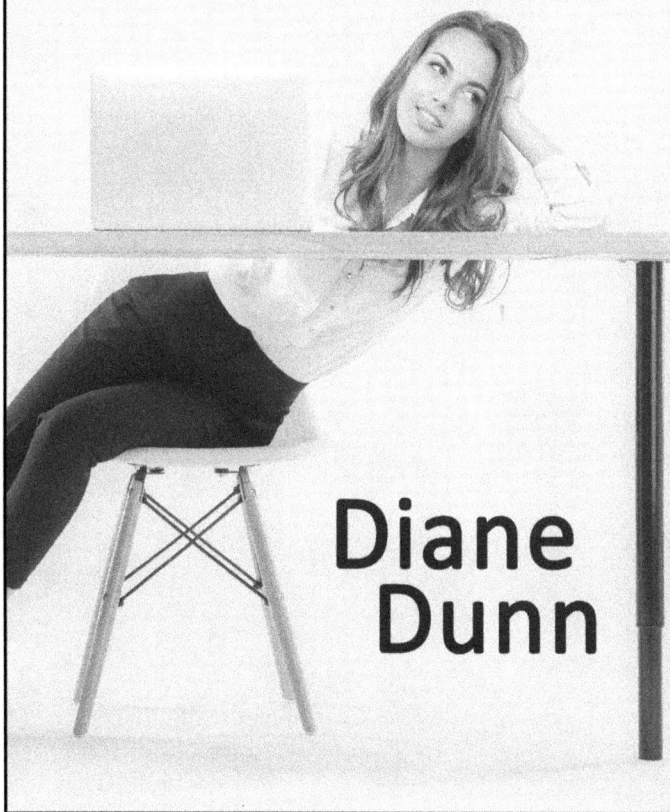

Organizing Your Home Office

For a More Successful You

Diane Dunn

Visit www.DianeDunn.org to order your copy today!